I0519001

# Ink Blot Girl

By Rose Ivy

Curious Corvid Publishing

*Ink Blot Girl* by Rose Ivy

© 2024, Rose Ivy

Published in the United States by
Curious Corvid Publishing, LLC, Ohio.

"Consume Self" originally published in the *Future Splendor* anthology
by Bee Infinite Publishing

Cover Art by Demar Douglas
Formatting and typeface by Ravven White

ISBN: 978-1-959860-36-5

Printed in the United States of America

Curious Corvid Publishing, LLC

PO Box 204

Geneva, OH 44041

www.curiouscorvidpublishing.com

First Edition

Curious Corvid
PUBLISHING

# Author Notes

Writing has been my whole life. It is not a hobby but what makes me feel complete. *Ink Blot Girl* is me navigating myself out of writer's block while simultaneously exploring different parts of myself. It is hard to be fully present in any given space, especially when you have so many elements of self to represent. This poetry collection honors elements of myself and acknowledges that my body deserves to take up space and share my voice.

Belonging has always been an alien feeling to me, but when I am writing, I am home. Ink Blot Girl is someone I run to when I am feeling lost. My collection does not follow any form, but I explore finding myself in each type of poem/prose within this book. This book reflects pieces of myself that have often been quiet or pushed to the side and is celebrating one of my favorite selves.

As you read these poems, be present, acknowledge the different layers that create you, think of your favorite self, and know that your voice is uniquely you and it can not be mimicked. You deserve the space you take up. Art can be healing and revealing.

# Table of Contents

## And the old me died.
## Ink Blot Girl is Born.

I was misplaced anger
and outstretched rivers.
The forgotten memories
within attics
and every drop
of water
that *slipped*
through wanting fingers.

I was all wind,
thunder,
and no storm.
Every eye to the sky
with no clouds in sight.
Curtains drawn
with pretty
satin bows
just begging
to be unraveled.
The show

that never showed.
I was all want
and no action.
Thoughts crashed.
Waves upon an
eggshell skull.

Enough words
to fill libraries
but I was all thought
and slivered tongues
left underneath a mattress.

I used to be
all smoke signals
and no fire.
*Now I am just fire.*

# My Dear Writer Girl

*"When I started out, I did compare myself to others. Was I good enough? Was I pretty enough for that role? But it's the impostor syndrome that is injected in any artist out there. What it does is it keeps you striving for excellence, and wanting to do better, and wanting to get it right even when you feel like you never hit it. Doubt keeps you in the process, and it keeps you honest."* — Viola Davis

*My dear writer girl,*
I know your heart races
every time your pen
swirls each letter.
That special pink pen
with the soft grips.
It must be soft grips,
you hold pens too tightly.
Imprints
staining tender
amber skin.
I know you feel
your heart

stop
at every sentence.
You are an
unending ink well.

But
when the well dries—
Let the pages mourn
your touch.
Lay your journal down
in a bed of roses,
but do not forget
the orchestra playing
in your DNA.
The beat of the drums
under the stars.
The rhythm of ancestors
dancing to music
through a moonless night.
Symphonies of language just waiting
beneath the surface of honey skin.

*My dear writer girl,*
give it time.
Some days

life takes it all
and on those days
the well feeds fire
into your resting soul.
The ink will never dry.

Do not bite your hand.
Do not throw
all your pens
out the cracked window.
Because
      your words
          are pieces
    of you
      on blank pages.

One day you will see
blooms of petals
in every color
sprouting
from wanting
mouths.
Sleeping and dreaming,
and dreaming
and dreaming.

Golden strings will grace
your divining hands.
Inkwells will burst
into oceans that lie
buried just beneath
the surface,
and you will live there
but you will not drown.
You will flood
pages
with self.
Write the words
that were stuck
between your teeth
waiting
to be unleashed.

*My dear writer girl,*
even when your pen stills
and your journals
rest there calling to you
upon a dead rose bed.
You are still a writer.
Not a shadow

with a mask
and weak wrists.

Wait until
your sun rises again.
You have always been
a garden blooming.
Everyone faces
cold winters,
icy veins,
slowed pens.

Wait—
until spring comes
and it always comes.
Those days will
make fat fairies
out of the muses
that are buried
in the marrow of your bones.

*I will be with you when that day comes.*

# Ink Blot Girl

Have you ever reflected
on the beginning of your life,
when all we had was dirt and a mouthful of seeds?

# Ink Blot Girl

# My mom doesn't know why I want to be called Rose.

"Terryn is a good name," she says.
I am named after my dad.
Just Terry with an N on it.

It was supposed to be "Taryn," which is the most
common spelling of the name but my mom was
rushed to emergency surgery because she lost
several quarts of blood and my dad made sure to
change it while the doctors were trying to save her
life and I struggled with underdeveloped lungs that
were gasping for air.

*I have always been gasping for air.*
*I was born with small lungs,*
*at least I had an excuse that day.*

My father was a wild card. Strong lion. Strong Leo.
He broke walls in my home so much so that we
always had to stucco. I know how to patch holes.
But only in walls. Only walls. The flesh that encases
us is too delicate.

I was called Kira in high school.
Some days it felt like I wanted to be the controller
of death or of my own fate. What is the difference?

My dad drunkenly let out my kitten a few years
back. He had just met his first new girlfriend since
the divorce, and she was a heavy drinker. My dad
had to keep up after all the years he had missed
from "being shackled".  My dad swore up and down
and called me a bitch for even thinking that he was
the one who let the cat out. His mouth smelled like
schnapps, and he was in yesterday's clothes. We
never talked about the cat again, but I swear I saw
the little thing three years later.

*Not so little anymore.*
*Looking strong.*
*People who leave that house*
*become strong.*

Terryn is a good name a boy once told me. He said
it was the name of aliens from *Star Trek* but I
found out years later that they were actually the
Earth people in the show. Why is it like me to

always feel grander than I am? Or to let someone tell me I am grander than who I am?

I became Wiccan. Aligned all my chakras and rooted myself to the earth. Terra is the earth. The name still didn't feel like home. I sat down and meditated while the Palo Santo burned, and I lost myself. I could not find the me in all the dirt. Or maybe I was the dirt? Even covered in dirt I am not that.

I landed upon Rose. It was a nickname brought on by a series of dreams after a manic fit. I ran away from home that year. I no longer felt like the death god or controller of my own fate. So, I took the name and every thorn that went with it. I wore a coat of thorns.

I know I have seen homes but have I been in one? Is there a definition for home? Is it as vague as the definition of a name? Do roses grow within my body? Is that not a house?

*A rose that never wilts isn't a rose but beyond that.*

My mom is a Leo too. She was a soft lion but had claws that you wouldn't see coming. She was a good hunter. Everything was prey to her. Ironic. Two lions with the wrong type of pride.
I think Leos are supposed to mean strong willed but in my parent's case they were and still continue to be two different types of assholes.

I never fucking believed in the zodiac anyway.

*Or the stars. Or a name. Or a house. Or a grander scheme of things.*

*A Rose is A Rose is A Rose.*

# Gasping and Grasping

*I feel as though I lost my ability to articulate. My language skills dwindling, I find myself to be speechless when I need to speak up. Maybe I need the silence, maybe my mind is trying to find places of calm within all the chaos of the world. How do people manage day to day? How do you breathe easy? Because I find myself gasping between breaths some days. The pressure slowly splinters my ribs and the oxygen around me flees, giving life to something else. Maybe the tender folds of my brain couldn't take the strain so my brain traveled deep into my subconscious for the winter. What started off as a migration for safety became the foundations of a home. I have tried to claw out but all I find is gray matter and chunks of earth.*

# Ink Blot Girl

# Ink Blot Girl no.666

It is like I live

and exist

in the margins

of someone else's story.


Written notes trying to find home maybe?

Am I the highlight of something important?

Spaces in spaces.

# Ink Blot Girl

# Writer's Block Brain—A Forced Number Poem

1. I heard numbers and words don't mix really well but I will give it a shot. I lost myself when math added imaginary numbers. Are there imaginary letters?

2. How dare I try to trap myself between numbers. Stuck in the structure of run-on sentences upon white pages. What if I have a side note? And then another side note? Does that get carefully placed under just like an outline?

3. I have hit a fucking wall. Or was it the corner of the page? I thought I knew what words were but I woke up eating a dictionary. The ink was blue but not blueberry flavor.

4. I thought I lost my pen. I have a habit of chewing on it when I get lost in thought. I woke up chewing my hand. I must have been having wondrous writer dreams. Why did I not take the time to find my pen so that I can dream while I am awake?

5.  I obsessively read other people's work and try to dissect their brain and words and compare them to my own. I never measure up. Seriously, I am ten steps away from *Misery*-ing my next favorite poet.
    a. I buy all their books.
    b. I dream of their faces while their words dance with clouds above me.
    c. I then stretch my words and shape them to my own. Leaping from one hand to another. They have all inspired my pen. Not my hand. My pen in hand.
6.  The "I believe I can fly" song only applied to me as a child.
    a. As time passed on, I could barely hear the melody.
7.  I am losing steam! Why are there so many numbers? There are so many words I need to look up. My dictionary is growing legs and hiding from me!
8.  I know that my pen and my muse ran away. Everything is running from me now.
9.  How do I find the energy to write? I remember sparks flying off of pages and I was

high off all of the good brain chemicals. They are better than the bottled ones. Artisanal brain chemicals.

10. I found my pen but all my paper is no longer white. Tainted by time, the colors have faded. Empty pages covering the surface of my lungs.

11. The traditionalist wouldn't call my writing "poetry" but I would like to have stiff drinks underneath bright moons and talk about our love of pens. I prefer black ink, every blue I have found is too soft. What happens if I want to write about the sky? I have a fear of things getting lost on paper.

12. How do I
    a. break apart
    b. structure?
       i. Is there a place for me
       ii. to fit between
       iii. the numbers or the curve of each letter?

13. It is hard to know my place.
    a. I just forgot how to *write* the word place. I spelled it wrong 10 times before I got the lettering to curve just right.

14. It is hard to know my place.

15. Being a writer is the best.

16. Being a writer is the best.

17. Until the day it disappears without a trace, making you question the very thing that made you whole. Not only whole but full, bloated, and complete.

18. I hope I never stop.

19. I hope I never.

20. I hope.

21. I.

# Call it Love

I am not so sure the majority of people understand *love*, such a simple four letter word we were taught at a young age. We have simplified the word into bite sized pieces rather than describing the gravitational effects on the soul. We have created a one dimensional word, devoid of the complexities and intricacies.

We romanticize *love*. What a beautiful thing to place up so high and to bask in. Why not enjoy all the feels that come with being swept up. Butterfly swollen bellies and occupied minds. Why not fall for the hazel eyed girl down the street? Place her as the leading role. Dream of her waltzing gracefully on the pedestal you placed on the roof of your home. Better yet, place her on the clouds. After all, the weight of the clouds is nothing compared to the weight threatening to burst open the walls of your heart. Yell at *love* as you fumble her in your hand. Wander your room and sit perplexed that *love* fell off your pedestal. That her ankles snapped. That she wasn't who you thought. No wings. No crown wrapped with silk and gold. A "no wonder" kind of girl like you dreamed of. Just a person. Just a woman down the street you never really met. Try placing those feelings elsewhere when *love* has abandoned and tricked you again. Tell her that you were too caught up by the flow of her dress and the waves of her hair. Call her a fool. A mirage. Scream to the skies that *love* is an illusion the worlds fall prey to. Now, *love* is something you don't believe in until the next wonder appears through a coffee shop door, or walking outside your window, or a smile walking through the cereal aisle. Call that meeting fate. Say that it is the rebirth of *love* in a different form. Call their smile karma long overdue.

Isn't it exhausting meeting your almost destiny, searching for them with every step? How do you feel when you crave something you no longer believe in? And after a kiss with sleep dust in your eyes, call it **love**.

- *To the only love that knows all of me*

# Ink blot girl Entry no.2929

I wear short clipped sentences.
(and. pretend. each. period. is. a. bullet. wound.)

I have attempted to write it out
but my pen has run out of ink.

I have left clues
between the spaces
of each line
and covered myself in
complex sentences
metaphors
and dream in allusions.

Always bleeding
ink
on blank pages.

# Ink Blot Girl

# Night Blindness

my tongue slips
i lose my grip
my skin covers
dry bones
and worn muscles

skin
porous
and cracked

my tongue slips
night shadows
dark corners
sense the danger
in the dark
when did i become
the villain?

when did i
start seeing
shadows
as a bad thing?

society calls me
dark
says i am a bad thing
when did night
slip in my mouth?

it's Tuesday
i am still a shadow
i wrote a story
the shadows
stole the ending

damn society
and my
soft mind
for burying me
in my own skin
sin
skin
skin living in sin
skin slipping
society hangs
by loose threads
or pressed
under concrete clouds

# Ink Blot Girl

skin slips sags into sin

shadowed night girl
known unknown
i wish i knew

# Ink Blot Girl

# Ink blot girl Entry no.589

Who teaches who
what canon is?
I am
a motherfucking
canon.
Dark like gunpowder.
Black girl magic
I am explosive.

Blowing holes
through
old textbooks.

The print was black
they
just didn't
see us
between
all the spaces
and white
pages.

# Ink Blot Girl

## Within you

I have too many eyes to count.
I am shattered in places I can't perceive
but when the sun is at its peak
you can see the holes that I smile through
create rainbows that dance around me.

I have lost my way
but I don't remember when
I took my first breath.
Does every journey have to have a climax?

I have fought against self,
and lost.
Why does there have to be a war?
Why are we our own worst enemies?
I know what switchblade tongues
and thorned hugs are.

I thought I was the light,
that I carried
the very energy of the morning—
but I am the shadow of the moon
and I am losing face.

# Ink Blot Girl

Why must I haunt self
to find the pen?
To search for myself in inkwells
while I am wounded.
And yes,
I am wounded.

My family searches for someone—
A mold of a girl.
A mold of a million girls
nestled and coiled into one.
Fragments and flashes
unmarked graves
embedded in my DNA.
I wake choking on funeral flowers.
Whose I don't know,
but I mourn just the same.

I have screamed love so many times
my mouth aches at making those shapes.
I don't know when
those words will be my last
so I say it five times in a conversation.
My heart pours and bleeds,
it wakes and aches

with the lives of too many to count.
Who am I now?

I am a ghost.
I am a ghost
of dead women.
So many dead women with no graves.
So many dead women whose bodies were property.
So many dead women who deserved to be saved.

I have swallowed every thorn,
but these wilted rose petal fingers
remained the same.
And this ink
just stains.

# Ink Blot Girl

# Ink Blot Girl no.0307

Some days
my pen
doesn't fit in my hand
and I have to
snap
and gnaw
at my fingers to even
jot down
a
sentence.

Yet—
other days,
it's as if my hand
is possessed
and I am sick.
Ailed by the written language.
Something that can only be cured
with a pen
scribbling on paper
for hours.
The other day,

## Ink Blot Girl

I dreamt I was a writer,
but I woke up
to find all my pens and
paper had disappeared.
Left to live their life.

# Re-Memory

I have always felt lost. A misplaced object on this vast planet. No land to call home. I did not have Goldie Lock's sense of comfort anywhere. My face, this body, an enigma to some, but I didn't know this vessel needed to be solved. My ancestors sprawl the entire globe, my blood calling to lands I have never stepped in, people who will never see me, never know of me. This pit in my stomach alerting me to all the other places that live in this body.

When I was younger, before my memories started to form (and then leave), call it an accident, say it was the mistake of a new parent—an iron met with my face as I crawled on the bed. Journeying through blankets alone. Soft flesh vs. the first touch of too much heat. I wonder how long I cried. My dad could only think of one way to remedy such a situation. (If you are thinking he took me to the hospital, you would be wrong and probably a responsible person). He bandaged my face and took me to the most magical place on Earth. Somewhere in a lost box is a picture of me, age two with my face surrounded in bandages to hide the swelling, as I attempted to smile in front of the Disneyland castle. He carried me all day through the park. Why did no one stop him and say something? Too busy being swept up by the most wonderful place on Earth, ignoring all the other natural wonders. As we took pictures, did he stop some random person and say, "hey, could you take a picture of my baby mummy and I?"

I wish I would have understood growing up, that my body was like that scar, out of place, a topic of conversation. Younger me should have known. I wish I could tell her to stop searching for home and cultivate a garden within her ribcage.

People still question that scar. My place and where I belong.

Now I just smile. Answers, no answers. I don't have to say anything. I only want to give myself everything.

Ink Blot Girl

*In a world full of bees,*
*I choose to be a rose.*

*Soft flower*
*petaled skirt*
*deceptively sharp.*

# Ink Blot Girl

## Broken Muse

**Curse my feelings and my wounded pride.**
I look at you as if we are standing
on two different planes,
and you are just a giant whisper.
My first beautiful muse,
you started a fire within my very core
and led me to wells of true passion.
I have grown and become a person
driven by the pen.

My memories of us
still gifting me a butterfly swollen belly,
and your touch was enough to keep me warm
until the last star burns out.

My passion for writing was a seed you planted
and it bloomed with your words.
My mouth poured fountains of ink.

Every page I wrote was just another dedication.
I have fashioned you a dress made out of books
I wrote for you.

# Ink Blot Girl

You,
my darling muse, gave me so much inspiration.
It felt as if the flow of it would never cease.
Even now, my pen has a mind of its own,
and I have to stop myself from writing your name
on such clean white pages.
You have caused a stillness in a hurricane that hides
just beneath my skin.
Your voice—
A direction.
A place to house all that chaos.

Who knew the English language
could be so freeing?

You loved the taste of chaos.
I gave you the taste of mayhem with the prick of my
pen.

You were all the forces of nature
I thought I could survive—
your tidal wave hair
pushing me over
again and again.

# Ink Blot Girl

When I graced your skin,
I felt the heat of a volcano.
I knew what it meant to be burned.

I stayed happy, putting you high
upon that chandelier.
You stayed there, lounging and at ease,
casting large shadows upon the walls.
I was too busy looking at something
that was not in focus,
being enchanted by your
honeysuckle scented presence.
Mesmerized by a label I gave you—
my muse.

You and passion are the same word to me.
I clumsily placed my happiness
and you
in the same breath.
Living to write
and living for you
blurred together
into one wild
primitive feeling.

# Ink Blot Girl

The angels have wept for a
foolish confusion of love.
I was unable to tell the difference between the two,
too busy falling for the imagery and concepts of a
muse,
I made a different clay version of you
with every poem.
And now I can build a tower,
a monument to you made from my sorrow.
If you listen, you can hear the sound of weeping,
my hand worn from the writing
and the clay moldings I made feverishly
in the moonlight.
You have built a tower around yourself now.
I wish I could have seen these
unmatched affections,
because I can feel that my passion is
burning right through me.
Together, we were a star that burned too bright,
and now I am scorched by the very thought of you.
You started this blaze,
but I am the one who has to learn
to let go and tend to the burns.

# I always take my morning walk at 9am.

There are not many people about and I can stroll slowly, soaking in the surroundings. Trying to be present. I have this issue with fading. I don't think there is a treatment for it.

I walk past this park. It's a small almost non-existent park, but everyday the same group of people sit at the blue metal benches. They laugh and I feel their rumble in my belly. I hear their words of poetry.
I always thought it was nice. A group of morning poets. I walk slow. Not slow enough to be noticed.

I do this everyday.
I have done this everyday for two weeks.
Everyday they are there.
Consistent morning poets. What a thought!
I wonder if they grew their words there or
did they carry them on their backs to this place?

# Ink Blot Girl

I heard one shout,
"Hello, hello"
but it was the beginning of this poem
that once got stuck between my teeth.
They must taste the same passion
that sprung from their pages and out through their vocal
cords like I did.
I would like to join
but my feet are insistent on moving
as much as mind.

I hear their beats and their clever lyrics. I want to
know what it would be like to be a morning poet
instead of a person who walks in the mornings.

# The Production Factory

## I. Sound

Airwaves moving backwards
and forwards through solids, liquids, or
gasses

> *the airways*
> *that move*
> *move around you*
> *create space*
> *take up space*
> *within you*

reaching towards ears

> *tender ears*
> *the one*
> *that shutters*
> *at the violence*
> *of silence*

The stronger the vibrations, the louder the
sound

> *somedays*
> *i am quiet*
> *others*
> *i am loud*
> *sometimes*

*too loud*
*mouth exhausted*
*and breathless*

Different frequencies and amplitudes create
variations of sound
Sound waves bounce off eardrums

*uniqueness of the voice.*
*have you heard me before?*
*can you hear me now writing these*
*words?*

## II. Creation of Sound

The body uses three different systems to
create sound.

1.  The Respiratory System is called
    breath support.
    This includes the lungs, ribcage,
    chest muscles, diaphragm, and
    windpipe.

    *breath is the fuel or power*
    *behind voice production*

2.  The Phonatory System also known
    as the larynx or the voice box is
    where sound is built. Vocal cord
    vibrations are the source of sound.
    *you can feel the growl*

50

*stretching over*
*your skin*
*building*

You close your vocal folds and begin
to exhale, causing an increase in
pressure that starts to vibrate.

*breath*
*pushes*
*sounds*
*build*

3. The Resonatory System, also known
   as the vocal tract, includes the
   throat, nasal passages, sinuses, and
   mouth.

*glide fingers*
*softly from*
*your torso to your face*
*so much power*
*packaged tightly*

The vibrations from the vocal folds is
what creates the human voice
through resonance which is the
shaping and amplification of the
sound waves of the vocal tone.

*do not continually crush*
*protect your swan neck*

*it houses something precious*

Ex. If you take a breath and hum for a few seconds, you will experience this sensation of resonance in the front of your face.

*"Meeeeeeeeeeeeeeeeeeeeeeee......"*

Once the Sound waves reach your mouth, you use your lips, teeth, and tongue to shape the sound into speech.

## III.   Speak

*the voice is power*

These organs all work automatically to create sound.

*you choose what to say
do you swallow them down*

or

Let the voice build in the diaphragm and move

*open your mouth and give it a try*

*SAY: "THIS IS MY VOICE.*

*The sound produced from
my fleshy body.
What a beautiful sound."*

Communication one mouth to another.

*sets us apart and builds worlds*

*speak*

# Ink Blot Girl

# Ink Blot Girl Entry no.4311

I don't know why writing was serious to me. Did I
think someone would be quoting me for the next
few centuries to come? Was I going to find a way to
break and bend a sentence in some revolutionary
sort of way? Give language wings? Take it on dates?
Buy cheap wine?

*Would our romance be public or private?*
*It doesn't matter.*

# Ink Blot Girl

Ink Blot Girl

*I haven't been able to put*
*what I want to say into words,*
*so I fall into the wonderland of these pages.*
*Locked tight in the corner of my mind.*
*It has always been my favorite place to go.*

# Ink Blot Girl

# (BLACKOUT)

I found myself in ███ autumn████
I can't remember███████████████
████████████thoughts ██████████
████████████████████████████████
always hiding.████████████████████
████████████████████████████████
███████████████████████████████best
self,████████████████████████████
████████████████████████████████
I always chase myself into a corner.████
████████████████████████████████
running in circles ████ you were a bright light. Your
voice ██████ I swallowed your melodies ██
████████████lay next to me. ████████
████████drinking in all that burned honey█
██████████████████ is better than
██ ██████ drowning. ██████████
█████████████████ How ███████
████ I am awake? ██████████████
████████████████████████ dreams
████ i thought we would share but didn't. ████
████████████████████████████████
████████████████████████████████
█████████ stop this whirlwind. Ready to let go████
████ live on ███ only in my dreams.

# Ink Blot Girl

# Not your Tongue. Not your Pen.

Have you ever wondered
who has said your sentences?
Sat in soft skin like yours.


Imagine an axolotl and giant nine-eyed Spider
Bunny playing *Sorry!* underneath the stars on a
Wednesday in Paris when they should be studying
for the bar exam.


*See.*


Not only was that a really funny image
but
it shows you the power of language.
The power that you possess.
What do you choose to do with your voice?


Is it to tell people to imagine an axolotl and giant
nineyed Spider Bunny playing *Sorry!* underneath
the stars on a Wednesday in Paris when they should

be studying for the bar exam?
Or is there something *more*?

# Favorite Self

*My favorite part of me*
*is neatly tucked*
*between white pages.*
*Finally,*
*a carefully*
*constructed*
*stain*
*dancing upon*
*straight lines.*
*She lives in those white clouds,*
*a no mess kind of gal.*
*That's a period,*
*not an ending.*
*If she sings of sorrows,*
*they are rivers of ink and not blood.*
*Her words—*
*like magic,*
*sentences painting landscapes.*
*No stutter kind of gal.*
*She is sure of herself here.*
*Her grace lives*
*in the swirl of her letters,*
*not her steps.*
*Today and every day—*
*I pick up the pen*
*and*
*give life to my most favorite self.*

# Ink Blot Girl

# Ink Blot Girl no.004

As a child, i used to eat paper.

i enjoyed the blank pages,
i sensed the opportunity,
the open pastures.

Some days i craved paper with ink,
beautiful white stained pages.
i was searching for a home.
Even my early days i craved
words,
begged for the knowledge
to bleed into my bloodstream
along with the ink.

i wish to kiss each
page
with my cherry
ink stained tongue.

# Ink Blot Girl

# Don't be a songbird.

Passions breathing—
the birth of ten trillion suns.
My hand moving at the speed of light,
muscle memory is all too familiar.
Cleansing my soul
between the spaces of each letter.

Did you write for her?
Him? Them?
Literally everything else but self?
Yes,
until my heartbeat stopped.
My hand atrophied
and my pen wandered
throughout wonderland.

I was lost,
and my muse
must have been slumbering.
Lost faith
like I lost hope.

My muse and I were born on the same day
and she could feel my stilled heart
stitched together, entangled
in broken dreams and lost love.
I became more thorns than rose petals.
I swam through pools of saltwater
and I forgot how to float.
Perhaps I lost the ability to float.

My heart snapped
like a twig in an overgrown forest
and the wind was knocked out of me.
But my soul kept swirling
like bottled hurricanes.
My mind raged on like the eye of all storms.

I had forgotten how to take in air
when my passions died,
when I lost my words.
When blank pages and
blank dreams became the same thing,
and my pen
and my soul
and every empty page
fell endlessly at the edge of the universe.

# Ink Blot Girl

I rocketed through the core of each
known planet in the galaxy
and they all whispered sweet words.
Languages beyond time!
And then,
I fell some more.

Until I found a light!
No, a star!
No, the sun!
I have no clue what to call her.
She already knows my name.
She was already the light parts of my smile.
Bright beams stream from her eyes
when we look at the mirror in the morning.

Do you write for her?
Yes!
My pen is hot!
Creating smoke signals upon untouched pages.
Muses leap from unopened skin to dance
around the flames.

Will you write for her?
Yes!

Past! Present! Future!
Past! Present! Future!
Past! Present! Future!
Past! Present! Future!


My hand will find hers,
and we will dance
where ink rains down
and forms
pools at our feet.
My hand will never tire.
My pen will never dry.
My love will never end,
only root deeper into the earth.

Ink Blot Girl

*Have you ever reflected*
*on the beginning of your life,*
*when all you had was dirt*
*and a mouthful of seeds?*

# Ink Blot Girl

# Ink Blot Girl no.204

Slippery wandering tongue
escaping parted lips.
I keep getting tripped on syntax.

In the mess of I,
find myself
trying
in all
sentences.

*Clumsy pens.*
*Clumsy hands.*

Where do I belong here?
And why is the English language so damn
constricting?

# Ink Blot Girl

# I need my pen.

I missed the feel of it in my hands,
like a dancer's muscles remembering the art.
Remembering the touch of it pressing down upon
the paper.

Digital journal,
an iPad with a fancy tech pen,
and jammed letters on
sticky notes left around
like love letters to self.
It's remembering my voice is present
in every drop of ink.
But it wasn't enough.
I forgot the inspiration,
the spark
was harder to hold on to.

But with a pen,
there is something about the
sounds of scrawling on pages.
My fingers finds hope
in a long lost dream I have been searching for.
It's like dancing on top of the highest clouds.

# Ink Blot Girl

*I am here.*
*I am god.*
*I see all*
*and I am probably high off the lack of oxygen.*
I know myself in ways I can't see on the ground
and with this pen and the pages in my journal,
I find home on top of these clouds.

I prefer it here,
dancing on top of water puffs.
They weigh heavy above us,
unsuspecting threats
that choose not to fall down on us,
all the while floating with grace

I want to be like this always.
Warmed by the ray's on top of fluffy clouds,
way too close to the sun.

Overjoyed by words on paper,
ink stained fingers,
a heart that's bursting open.
Every seam I have stitched,
now the loops of my letters.
I am ready for blank page journeys!

# Ink Blot Girl

And tired feet from all the dancing!
Soaked shoes from the clouds,
soaked paper from the ink.

and a smile that lasts.

# Ink Blot Girl

*Is it the frailty and softness of rose petals that people admire or is it the bite of thorns across curious fingers?*

# Ink Blot Girl

# Enough

Call my breathing a testament
to survival
and my steps, stubbornness.
Each loop of the pen is where I live,
and I only see in ink blots.

I have been left gasping at night alone and scared,
but now I see the moon light shine down through
the trees,
while the wind flirts with the leaves.
Call this air in my lungs undrowning.

My steps are lighter each day.
Some will say I am floating,
but really I am walking small steps,
and that is enough.

-   you are enough.

# Ink Blot Girl

# Ink Blot Girl Entry no.415

*What is with the complexity of*
*writing?*

*Art blooming in the shadows.*
*How can we release the worry,*
*become naked,*
*Accepting of wandering eyes?*

*How do you not feel art wanting to live?*
*to speak,*
*to be tasted,*
*to be seen*
*to be thought of?*

*Why does the artist's mind torture itself?*
*Unsure minds,*
*uncertain words*
*launching from slowed tongues.*

*I would like to shine,*
*to be naked and bare upon these blank pages.*
*No shame,*
*no second guessing.*
*just the two of us consuming art.*

# Ink Blot Girl

## Truth within a Name

She is light in a
body of flesh.
Blood, bone,
muscle and sinew
packaged
in amber skin
that cannot
contain her light.
The first light.
The last light.

She has been here before,
learned to walk a thousand times,
always learning the life lesson too late
on when to silence her switchblade tongue
and still her trigger pen kept in back pockets.

Her palms have landed in prayer
but the gap in her hands
has left them unanswered,
trickling hope between nimble fingers.

Bruised knees before

satanic dreams of the past.
She wakes to
an unending nightmare,
fighting like any other.
You would not know
this
is a warrior's smile.
Someone who houses her dead
and wounded
beneath her rib cage.
      She is a Mausoleum
to lifetimes of memories
she does not have access to.
The key has been lost
in deep blue oceans.
Long days she
dreams of them
and wakes
covered in
dead
red roses.

Her bones creak and
you can saw her in half
and count the rings.

# Ink Blot Girl

Snap her branches.
For house.
For warmth.
For structure.
Just because.

Her life propels beyond this body.
The glow of her soul peaks through
when her mouth opens.

How she wants to be seen.
How she wishes to be called
by her true name.

A delicate flower.
Bruised and scraped,
yet flowing in the wind.
Sharp thorned tongue
and deep roots.

The universe knows her name.
Thorns and all.

Do you believe in the day you were born?

# Ink Blot Girl

# Ink Blot Girl Entry no.13

My mouth wrenches open
but there are no screams
living in my belly.
Sweat pouring from skin.

My sleep paralysis demon
knows of silence.
Consumes voice during slumber.
I swear
I saw
my
sleep demon
in the mirror
this morning.
Every morning.

One day I will sleep when I am awake
because sleep is where dreams are housed.
I try to wake and dream simultaneously
and I have fallen every time.

So,
I need to trick the mind.

The mind is a tricky thing.
Something about
the subconscious
and conscious.

I must
master sleep walking.
Sleep while awake
not walk with funeral flowers.
This is not practice
for an eternal slumber.

No,
I want to daydream.
I need to daydream.

*My mouth will gape open and a roar will be*
*growing.*

*Some days my phone auto-corrects Rose to Rise and I have never felt such a storm in my soul trying to break free.*

# Ink Blot Girl

# Dreams Speak or they don't
# – Part one

*Can a voice be possessed?*
*Owned by the softness of skin?*
*Did you know*
*skin*
*is the largest organ of the human body?*
*Is that a big enough container for the voice?*

*I think that I woke up falling.*
*Or was I naked?*
*My bare face*
*and arms flailing*
*like wings*
*hitting*
*silk sheets before*
*sunrise.*
*Why do I always wake before sunrise?*
*Can two fiery souls*
*not be birthed at the same time?*

*I always feel the dull panic*
*or the echo of something missing*

*or something I am forgetting.*
*If you have no voice in your dreams, is a future*
*possible?*

# Voids in Dreams

Honey ink tears
turn into solid crystal pools.
A silent haven where
I watch fish fly through salt water.
A celestial spectacle
embodied within every moment.
I wish to
ingest every piece until my eyes burst.
I see
wandering empty eye socketed animals
grazing peacefully
for they have consumed it all.

Here I write.
I write until I have no pages left.
I think I have found my forever home
within this soft blue pen.

Beside these crystal pools,
I empty.
Inside these blank pages,
I empty.

I crack ribs
and begin to fill the void.
I will bleed ink
until there is no more.
*No more ink.*
*No more void.*
*No more me.*

I wish to create new dreams.
Creating new dreams within dreams
that are unknown to me!
This makes me want to sing!
Oh, how I want to sing and sing!
Until there is no tune to carry.
I want to sing!
And sink.
And sing and sink.
To grow roots into fertile soil.

Growth is
where my dream leads.
Falling backwards
down the rabbit hole.
Me and gravity dancing.
Gravity is doing

a graceful tango.
Until it stops.
Until it bleeds
*and dies*
*like mortals do.*

# Ink Blot Girl

# Dreams speak or they don't – Part two

Some dreams are about being late to work or falling over and over again. If only my dreams were rooted in simple forgetfulness of time or the weightlessness of freefalling through lost clouds with butterflies in your stomach. I always wanted to know the dream metaphor behind those things, but I never picked up a book on it. Something about a dream in a dream. Subconscious within the conscious. Unsure, really.

No, my dreams revolve around me losing my voice. Mid conversation, when waking up, while dreaming in dream. I loved the *Little Mermaid* when I was younger. I wonder if that has anything to do with it. Did I admire a woman losing her voice and then becoming queen? Do I have to find my voice to gain nobility? Can someone like me be noble? I used to fear losing my voice so much that I signed up for sign language classes but never went. I make sure to scream the lyrics in my car when I am driving alone. I scream like no one can hear me or until I can't hear me. My voice grows hoarse on long drives. Too much of me in small spaces. Who taught me I was too much? I think it was my mother. Did her mother tell her the same thing? Has it truly been generation after generations of women telling women to lessen themselves, to shrink into small spaces?

Once my friend and I were watching funny videos on YouTube. A family was playing a practical joke on the youngest daughter. They pretended she was invisible while she stood in the middle of the room. Her face went from laughing to panicking instantly. Her tears streaming down her face were interrupted by the booming laughter of my friend. He enjoyed the joke. I looked at the tv screen as if I were looking into a mirror. Tears streaming down my face. I knew what it was like to be invisible and ignored. It was no joke. My tears were silent. His laughter filled the room.

In one dream I spent the day trying to talk to anyone who passed me. I swear I woke up with a new cluster of gray hairs upon my head and clutching at my throat. There were claw marks. It seems like something was trying to get out. Maybe something was trying to get back in? Some things are easier to accept in dreams. Something about the subconscious within the conscious.

I was talking to my mom about the ending to the movie *Shape of Water*. My recent obsession. I think I was attached to the character because she was voiceless. Such beautiful melodies and feelings translated all without words. Weird, it's like I have the inability to look into a mirror. I think I broke all my mirrors in October one week after staring at my yellow wallpaper until my eyes crusted over. The veil was way too thin. I heard whispers one night as I passed them. The sound was so familiar, that I spent the rest of the night breaking every mirror with a hammer. I know someone was trying to get out! To be heard! I knew what that was like. Anyway, my mom didn't understand the ending. How did she miss it? The main character was literally a flipping mermaid I shrieked. My voice cut off and the more I tried to talk the more air that escaped my belly and became life support to some nearby hot air balloon. Why couldn't she see what was right in front of her? The character was never drowning. Not at the end.

I dreamt of the character No Face for a month after I watched *Spirited Away*. I turn to look over my shoulder at nights hoping to see them peering behind the corner. I understand them. I resonate with a silent spirit perceived to be a monster with no words, destroying things and trying to give, pure chaos and destruction, until someone sees me, until someone finds a way to help my silent suffering. Some days there is just no one there to help and you only have yourself to fight the chaos. Who taught me what chaos was? Where did I learn control or how to destroy? Is it destruction if it's silent?

How did Ariel's voice feel in the seashell? Was the shell container similar to Ariel's salt covered throat? Did it prefer the difference in location? Did it care to be home or did it even know that Ariel was its home? I wonder why women's voices are preferred to stay in soft shells. How does one harden an eggshell body that has been cracked? What is so damn angelic about fragility? In something that can be crushed beneath a thumb. What is the definition of fragile? Who defined the word? Did a man define it? Was he thinking of soft skins and pink lips? Did he think fragility was beautiful or did he dissect it piece by piece under a dull blade?

*I would like not to be the type of fragile that expands like bruised rose petals in lungs but fragile like a field of landmines, ready to bloom at any moment.*

# Ink Blot Girl

*I bit my tongue*

*...*

*and tasted all my lost words*

# Ink Blot Girl

# Consume Self

*It's that dream again.*

*The only dream I have had since that night.*

*My only reprieve is that most nights are black. My eyes close and I fall under blankets of black. In that state, I am at the most peace.*

*It's a haze during the day and I don't feel the touch of my skin anymore. I have spent the past month in silence. Silently, moving from place to place in my room. Haunting my hallways. At first my silence was easier than talking through the tenderness of bruised flesh but after a while the silence was home.*

*I suspect people have called but I don't have the energy to check my phone. If I were to check, I would have to admit how much time has passed. I will have to give room for more room. I must make the "right steps" my last therapist said.*

*But tonight, or today, the blackout curtains have remained closed, so I am unsure of what time it is. I have spent my days listening to music with no words and let the wordlessness soothe me.*

*My unmoving body melted into sheets. I was welcomed by darkness as the violin cried in the background.*

*No, it was that dream again.*

*I wake. Or I think I am awake. There is a dirt road that leads to a giant red tent. Or maybe a soft flesh cavity. I know this road led to a big red tent and nothing else. I have been here before. It is my only dream now and there has never been anything else. In the tent is a series of mirrors and hallways with more mirrors. I hate it. I always panic. Too much me within tight spaces so I run. I have run every time speeding through hallways and hitting dead ends, ones where a different me is looking at me.*

*Tonight is different though. I heard Aurora sing outside my window today.*

*The silent ones are my choir*
*The sea waves are my evening gown*
*And the sun on my head is my crown*
*I made this queendom on my own*

♪ ♪

*Her sweet song had been the first words I had*
*heard in what seemed like years. Did she bring*
*new dreams with her as she walked past?*

*The pathway led to the big red tent but instead of*
*the normal panic, I heard her gentle tune.*

*The silent ones are my choir*
*The sea waves are my evening gown*
*And the sun on my head is my crown*
*I made this queendom on my own*

♪ ♪

*I walked in the middle of the tent and faced the*
*many faces of me that I had been running from*
*dream after dream.*

*Before I knew it, my hand was gliding through the
first mirror. Pieces scattered on the ground and I
expected blood. I expected wounds. But instead,
each face of me crawled beyond the mirror.*

*The tune faded into a starless night.*

*Their eyes searching and pleading.
No more running. No more panic. You are in
pieces, they said in unison.*

*And in the blink of an eye,
the tent was a balloon fading into the sky.
And I and my many selves,
sit in a garden surrounded by wild rose bushes.*

*Ink Blot Girl—She sits in a burgundy velvet dress
and a black knit sweater drinking Jasmine tea.*

Her voice started
when there was nowhere to turn.
No one was listening.
Her father was a lion.
Her mother was a lion.
All she knew was the taste of blood.

# Ink Blot Girl

She spilled ink onto willing pages.
Grieved and melancholic
words were her only vocabulary.
She spent days loving a language
that no one saw.
Underneath teal satin covers,
she wrote worlds.
Until,
her words slowed.

Language ran from her
when she lost herself.
Escaping within
other soft bodies
that knew nothing of
art.
Such an all
or nothing type of person.
When writing she is whole.
When the pen stops,
she stops.
The end.

The unwritten notebook
paper slowly built her a coffin.

# Ink Blot Girl

Her words dimmed.

Her pen stilled.

She waited for the light to come back.

> *My dear Ink Blot Girl,*
> *I will eat the*
> *unused hand you complain of.*
> *I will break each bone and*
> *simmer them slowly in a stew.*
> *The left hand holds creativity*
> *not sin.*
> *Fires are kindling.*
> *Soften your heart*
> *and sit patiently.*
> *Everything that is holy is at the tip of your pen.*
> *...*

*The Lover—She floats on top of an overflowing ink well. Her chest glows and you can hear centuries of symphonies roar within her ribcage.*

At church she shrank,

cringed at the testimonials.

She tried to find the love between the pews.

*"You eating cupcakes?"*

her mother spat.

All love was not love to her.

Remembering the

taste of frosting

warming her lips,
driving in silence the rest of the way.
She shrank into her seat,
not wanting to go into detail about *her*.
The *her* she loved.
The *her* that took up volumes
of journals in her closet,
leaning closer and closer every time
she opened the door
threatening to crash down upon her.
When the love stopped,
so did her writing.

She found a grouping of similar people.
They loved outside the lines.
Their love was pure love in her eyes,
righteous and holy like any other,
somewhere she thought she could belong.
She wanted to know
what love was
and bloom.
There were moments
when that was enough.
Her gay friend once said
*You are greedy. You are indecisive.*

*I would never trust or date a bi or pan person.*
He was the first of similar voices that she
thought echoed her own.
But found they were not quite her.
Why was it so hard to find home?
She stood there with an empty belly
and she shrank.

*My dear Lover,*
*I will take your overflowing heart.*
*Your capacity to love is pure.*
*Love will always be pure.*
*You are more petals than thorns.*
*I shall deep fry your heart*
*in every beloved pan I own.*

...

*The Stain—She sits straight with her legs crossed,*
*wearing pearls and her edges done. Her foreign*
*tongue stands apart from her family.*

She has been called a token more times than she
can count. She fits in "odd" places where people do
not expect her. She is not brown enough to be an
Oreo, so her friend joked that she was a coconut.

She is a clumsy person. Tripping on self and words,
yet every stranger who meets her insists upon her

skill. Looking at her like a tall skyscraper—surely she loves basketball.

*You are really smart for a black girl.*
*You are really pretty for a black girl.*
Something said on repeat like a broken record.
Neither time or wokeness has changed perception.

*Black people don't have anxiety. That's a white*
*people thing that was made up,*
her dad said coolly while shoveling mint chip ice cream in his mouth.

She is usually the only person of color in her classes. Sometimes she swallows the feeling of being a space in someone's quota. It is hard to see accomplishments when an imposter sits upon your face like a mask, blocking your vision. Gasping for air, this is not what drowning feels like.

> *Dear Stain,*
> *your flesh like honey.*
> *I shall consume*
>
> *your skin and admire*
> *your melanin magics.*

...

*Mutt Self—Her face like Frankenstein's monster.*
*Piece by piece she is strung together.*

She is an enigma people have said, studying pieces of her face like an ethnic puzzle. Their faces illuminate when they think they have solved it. It is as if she has a teddy bear in her pocket, waiting to give to those who succeed in their guesses. Her face is not a game nor a prize.

*She has been haunted by the unknown.*
*The unknown of a large family.*
*The unknown of where family resides.*

Her dad was adopted in Germany, an enigma like her, yet he was adopted by a black couple and that was all he knew. All his questions stayed buried underneath skin where they boiled.

*He was always boiling over. So much anger at questions that were never asked and will never be solved.*

*His face held every unknown mystery swirling in
her blood but there were no roots, no traces, and
no paths.*

She invited her dad to Thanksgiving with her in-
laws. Her mother-in-law sat quietly, analyzing her
father's face. After he left, her mother-in-law's face
lit up and she was thrilled to tell her she was going
to buy her an ancestry DNA test for Christmas. It
was killing her not to know what her dad or what
she was. She turned out to be a hell of a lot of
things.

*She has been haunted by the unknown.*

Her mother-in-law studied her chart and the long
list of pedigree and frowned. "You aren't much of
anything." Her puzzled face seared into memory,
looking between her results and the missing pieces
she would never completely understand carved into
her bones.

> *Dear Mutt self,*
> *I will drink your blood.*
> *I will claim home*
> *to all your lands and I will smile.*

*I will blend a smoothie,*
*a cup*
*overfilling with*
*the pieces from Nigeria*
*the pieces from the Congo*
*the pieces from England*
*the pieces From Mali*
*the pieces from Norway*
*the pieces from Scotland*
*the pieces from the Senegal*
*the pieces from Togo*
*brilliantly*
*blending within amber skin.*
*Yes, you are a mutt*
*but your ancestors*
*spread across the Earth.*
*They all watch,*
*sending you love.*

...

*Bipolar Wonder—A woman jumping and crying in*
*the corner. Tears streaming down one side of her*
*face whilethe other side tries to contain a wide*
*smile. Her voice is caught between a sob and a*
*laugh. She doesn't know how to communicate to*
*others really.*

"My boyfriend is a Gemini. *He is so bipolar.*" She
twists in her seat and wonders how a zodiac symbol
has become the poster child of bipolar disorder.

There were times where she couldn't sleep for a week. Pacing became second nature. Feeling electric or that every blood cell within her carries a different pulse. She is teeming with energy and some days she is just way too fucking excitable. You can see her squirming, speeding as if time were chasing her.

There were times where she cried for days with no end and not knowing a reason. She just felt consumed. Listening to the same song by Natalia Kills on repeat. The one burrowed into her core. The one where she let the tune carry her for hours on end.

*I heard the angels call again*
*I threw myself a party*
*Chardonnay and oxy*
*I stopped the screams inside my head*
*You know devils don't fly (fly, fly)*
*So don't expect me not to fall*
*Devils don't fly (fly, fly)*
*You know that life ain't fair sometimes*
*Devils don't fly (fly, fly)*
*But I try*

She was always told that the mind can be a
dangerous thing. The mind can be a place of evil.
So, she fashioned herself into a villain. Took
comfort in the darkness before anyone could point
her out. She turned her body to cement and
anchored herself to the floor, losing track of time.
She tried to listen to voices of reason within these
moments, but she lost momentum before she even
started every time.

*Dear Bipolar Wonder,*
*I will consume your cycling feet.*
*They bleed and grow tired*
*because you have been*
*falling up hills and speeding down them.*
*Abnormal psychology has made you a ghoul.*
*Neurodivergence is who you are.*
*No abnormalities for the naturally occurring.*
*You are not a curse word*
*or something to be feared.*
*Cast aside the doubts that your body is a prison.*

*...*

*Survivor—She clutches onto a bow and arrow*
*standing in pools of her blood.*

She has survived.

    Drunken attempt of murder.

    Soft shelled head

hitting oak floorboards.

Sexual assault.
Stolen
not given.

Mental health issues.
Born and nurtured.

Chronic pain and nausea.
Car crashes and
twisted spines and
migrained mind.
Vertigo steps.
Movement
within movements.

Yet she wakes.
She exists.
And she persists to exist.

*Dear Survivor,*
*I will take your spine.*
*Freeze it and eat it piece by piece.*
*I need your strength when I forget myself.*

...

*The Sun—She is a silent ball of light illuminating the garden. She floats above the wild roses, watching us all. She watches me lovingly consume each piece. Creating a home for us all within honey skin.*

I am full.

Soft petaled skin.

Belly ripping at the seems,

smiling like a fool while looking into the mirror

learning to love the flow and ebb of the soul.


They are within me

and we are

mosaics of sorts,

symphonies of sorts,

gardens blooming within

skin.

# Ink Blot Girl

She woke up and
black clung to her
birth.
Black ink blot girl.
Such a stain.

She woke up
and her eyes dripped
blue.
Blueberry wonder
without the flavor.
Blue ink blot girl
crying oceans
onto blank pages

She grew
and she burned
like the sun.
Red ink blot girl
knew how to start fires.
Passion burning like the
first fire.

Ink blot girl.
A stain
nobody
could have guessed.
Someone who could
not be contained in pages
or the spaces between words.
Ink blot girl rests within
periods.

*Ready for a beginning.*

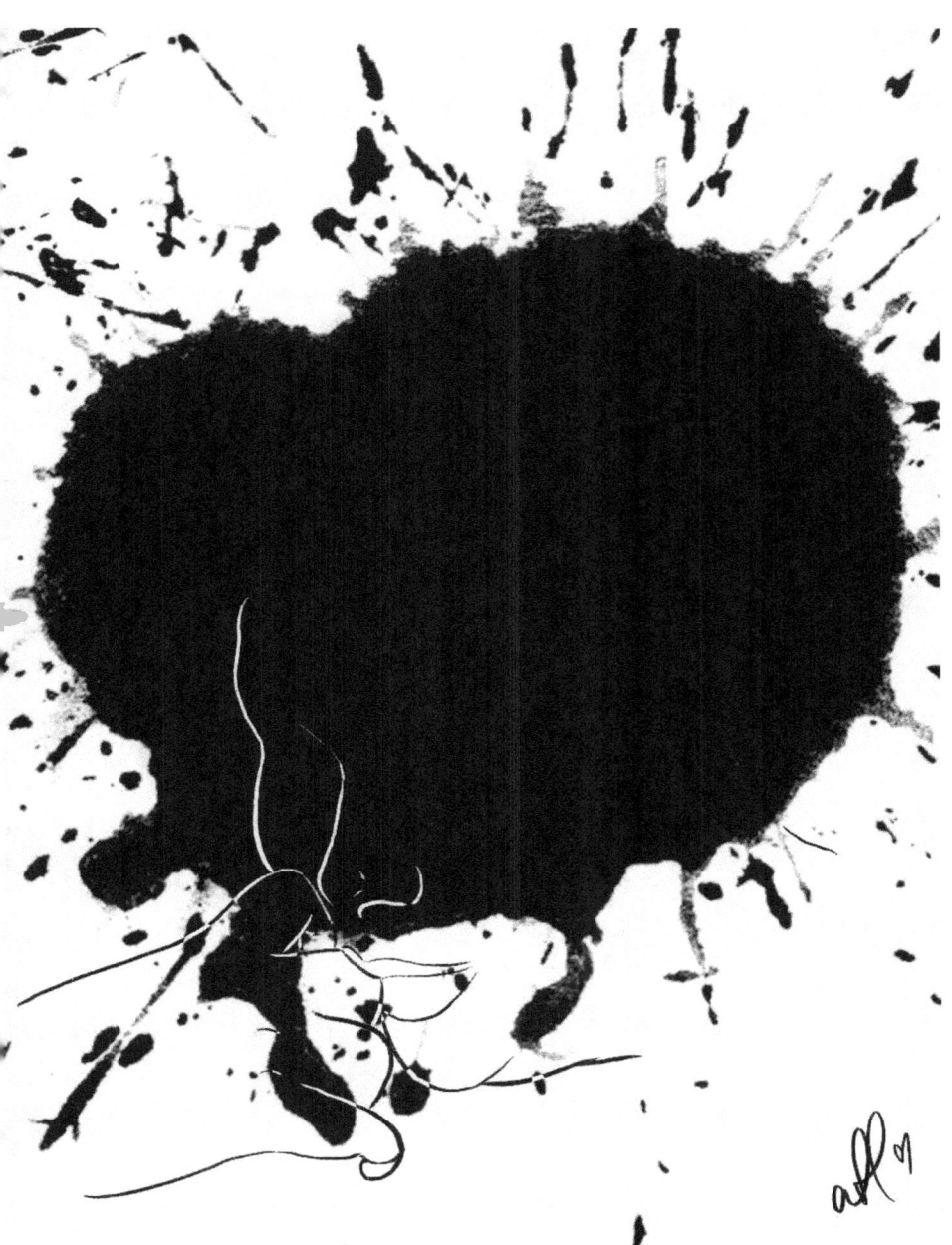

# Ink Blot Girl

# Acknowledgments

**First, I want to thank everyone who is holding this book.** I hope my words touched you in some way. When I started writing these acknowledgments, I stared at a blank page, not knowing how to express how much they all meant to me properly. This has been the first time I have had to sit down and write about the people who surround and love me in this life. I have been so grateful for the wonderful people in my life. Thank you all for loving the weirdo I am.

**To my husband,** thank you for showing me what unconditional love looks like. I didn't know how much my soul was looking for that type of comfort.

**To my amazing friend Ari,** I would have never had this book if you hadn't pushed me to continue writing in high school. Thank you for reading my words and writing with me all these years.

To Alyssa, thank you for your critical eye. Your commentary and feedback have been so important to me throughout the years. Thank you for creating with me. I hold those moments close to my heart.

To Courtney, thank you for always being there, always supporting me, and being the magical person you are.

To Rachel, your kindness and light shine brighter than any crystal I have seen. I have loved and continue to love every laugh-filled moment.

To Allyson, high school seems worlds away, but I am so thankful to have stayed close. Your kind heart will always be an inspiration.

To my Dad and my Aunt Nina, thank you for loving my art, even when you didn't understand what was written. Thank you for every gifted journal and for all the supportive words you gave me.

To the creative writing professors at Pitzer and Scripps College, thank you for supporting and sharpening my writing skills. You never know how much belief can mean to someone.

Finally, thank you to Ravven and everyone at Curious Corvid Publishing for believing in my words, for all the work you put into this book, and for helping me make my dreams come true.

# About The Author

Rose is a true eccentric and oddball. As a black sheep,
she has dedicated much of her life to writing.
At Pitzer College, she discovered the thrill of igniting
creativity in others. She believes the
wonderland of your mind can be explored by
experiencing and creating art. After obtaining her
master's degree in library and information science, she
divides her time between writing and
cherishing moments with her four dogs and two cats
when she's not immersed in literature.
*Ink Blot Girl* is her debut collection of poetry.

www.ingramcontent.com/pod-product-compliance
Lightning Source LLC
Chambersburg PA
CBHW071158120626
46546CB00006B/2317